Granny Han's Breakfast

SHEILA GROVES

An OMF Book

GRANNY HAN'S BREAKFAST

© OMF INTERNATIONAL
(formerly China Inland Mission)

Published by Overseas Missionary Fellowship (USA) Inc.
10 W. Dry Creek Circle, Littleton, CO 80120

First published 1985
Fifth printing 2005

ISBN 1-929122-15-2

OMF Books are distributed by
OMF, 10 West Dry Creek Circle, Littleton, CO 80120, USA
OMF, Station Approach, Borough Green, Sevenoaks, Kent TN15 8BG, United Kingdom
OMF, PO Box 849, Epping, NSW 2121, Australia
OMF, 5155 Spectrum Way, Bldg 21, Mississauga, ON L4W 5A1 Canada
OMF, PO Box 10159, Auckland, New Zealand
OMF, PO Box 3080, Pinegowrie 2123, South Africa
and other OMF offices

Illustrated by Drew Thurston

Contents

CHAPTER 1

Granny Han

They all called her Granny Han—"Han Po Po" in
their Chinese language, for she was no longer in
America but Taiwan. Pauline didn't mind a bit.
She was so delighted that all these young people
from the church and the university should enjoy
coming to see *her*—an older lady, and a foreigner
at that—and enjoy talking to her about
themselves and about her God.

"Han Po Po!" said the leader of the student group one day. "However are you going to get enough money for all the summer meetings that we've planned?"

Granny Han smiled. "Trust God for it!" she said. "He showed us it was right to have the meetings, so He will make sure we have enough money."

"It would be easier to charge everyone a fee for coming," said the young man doubtfully.

Granny Han shook her head. "No," she said firmly. "That would mean no one with a big family could afford to come. Don't forget what it says in your Bible, 'My God shall supply all your needs'—that means every last penny! And shall I tell you something else? Only this afternoon, several people came to me with gifts of money, so God has begun to answer our prayers!"

What Granny Han didn't tell the young man was that the money—including her own allowance for the next three months—had arrived half an hour *after* the banks closed. It was Saturday. What was she to do with the money over the weekend? She tried hiding it in different places all over the house, but somehow she didn't feel happy about it. So she changed all the hiding places again and snapped another padlock on the door. Now perhaps the money would be safe!

CHAPTER 2

Every Last Penny

As Granny Han came home from her meeting with the student group, she met her next door neighbor.

"Your little dog's come to meet you," remarked the neighbor as Cinderella came bounding down the path. "How nice!"

Nice? No, thought Granny Han suddenly, this time it was *not* nice. Cinderella had been firmly locked inside the house when she left ... Something was wrong! She made her way to the front door. Suddenly she realized that the sliding door was half open.

And the locks were broken.

Her heart pounding, Granny Han looked around the bedroom and the living room, her eyes seeking out the places where the money had been hidden. Many things had been moved, some piled high on her bed. In a flash she knew that it

7

was all gone. Every last penny.

Granny Han called to her neighbor and asked him to report the robbery. Then she sat down, thinking.

Strange that, though the job had been done in a hurry, things hadn't been thrown around but piled up neatly ...

Did the thief know the house?

Strange that it had happened tonight ...

Did the thief know she had all that extra money there?

Strange that the neighbors hadn't heard Cinderella bark ...

Did the thief know her little dog?

Strange that all the money had been taken except for the envelope marked "House-helper's salary"...

Could the thief be ....? Surely not. Granny Han tried to put out of her mind the possibility that it might be her house-helper, Oo-lan.

What was she to do now? She remembered what she had told the young man earlier that day—"My God shall supply all your needs"—and God never goes back on His promises, she had added. Quietly, Granny Han accepted the challenge. She would prove that the God of Abraham, Isaac and Jacob was her God too. She really would have to start depending on God for everything now. Not so difficult, perhaps, to trust Him for her own needs, for they weren't many. But what about the money for the conferences? That was enough to make anyone's faith take a nose-dive. And yet Granny Han was surprised to discover she felt completely peaceful about everything. She was certain that her God would take care of all her needs ... yes, every last penny!

But one thing more was necessary ...

Granny Han could not accuse Oo-lan of the robbery. She had no proof. But she couldn't help feeling very concerned for the girl.

"Lord," she prayed, "*I* do already believe that you are faithful and true—but please show Oo-lan that you are too! Let *her* see that you are the one, almighty, faithful God!"

CHAPTER 3

Bread from Heaven

"And when she got there, the cupboard was bare," Granny Han hummed to herself as she went to her old Chinese wind-cupboard not long after. She didn't have a fridge. But then, she didn't need one, living as she did on all-Chinese food. That meant shopping every day, and not keeping much food in the house. So the wind-cupboard—a small food cabinet with wire mesh round three sides and at the top so the cool wind could blow through—was usually quite enough.

A good way to live, normally.

But now, with no reserve of food, and no money to buy more, the cupboard really was almost bare.

It was the third day after the robbery when Oo-lan came early in the morning to Granny Han and said, "There's nothing in the house for breakfast!"

"Well, set the table anyway," Granny Han told her.

"Why should I set the table when there's nothing to eat?" grumbled Oo-lan, not looking at her.

"Set the table!" repeated Granny Han, more sternly than she meant to. "It's hardly eight

o'clock yet, and I usually don't breakfast till 8:30."

Mumbling and grumbling, Oo-lan started to slam down the breakfast things on the table. Granny Han slipped out, went to her bedroom and closed the door behind her. Then she knelt by her bed.

"Well, Lord," she said, "this is it! I really don't care if I eat or not ... you know what you want for me, and that's all I want. You promised to supply all my needs—but I can't pretend breakfast is a *need* at the moment, as I'm not exactly starving! But Lord, I'm asking you to show Oo-lan that you can provide for me...."

When she returned it was about 8:20, and Oo-lan was still fussing and complaining. Just then she heard someone knocking. Whoever could be calling so early? Granny Han went to open the door, and standing there was her neighbor, Mr. Li. Now Mr. Li came from Shandong, and that's where they make the best steamed bread in the whole of China. And now Granny Han's eyes nearly popped out of her head, for what should Mr. Li be holding out to her but an enormous plateful of steaming hot bread!

"For you, Han Po Po! We know how much you like our *mantou*," he explained, "and we made a specially big batch this morning so that we could give you some."

Granny Han thanked him, hardly able to contain her joy and excitement at God's answer to her prayer, and carried the steaming plateful indoors.

"Where did you get *that*?" Oo-lan asked in amazement.

"The Lis down the lane made it," said Granny Han simply. "Mr. Li just brought me some."

But Oo-lan seemed unimpressed. "You can't eat just steamed bread by itself," she objected.

"Well, lots of people do—and anyway, it will keep body and soul together." Granny Han sighed. What more did the girl need to convince her?

CHAPTER 4

Not by Bread Alone

Scarcely had Granny Han finished speaking when there came another knock—this time at the back gate which was never normally used. Whoever could *this* be? Granny Han made her way out to the back, leaving Oo-lan eyeing the bread suspiciously.

There at the gate stood little Mrs. Wang, and in her hands she carried a good-sized bowl. She was always rather nervous and excited, and now her hands were really trembling as she handed the bowl to Granny Han.

"I laid them myself!" she explained, her voice

shaking as much as her hands.

Granny Han took the bowl wonderingly and with great care. Inside were twenty eggs!

When she took the eggs indoors, Oo-lan couldn't believe her eyes.

"Who brought those?" she asked, her voice lacking some of its earlier scorn.

"Little Mrs. Wang, the one who has seven daughters," said Granny Han. "She said she laid these eggs herself, so they must be something special!" she chuckled.

But Oo-lan was not so easily won over.

"You still don't have any fruit or coffee," she insisted.

Feeling bolder now, Granny Han said, "We don't really need fruit every day, Oo-lan, and if the Lord thinks I should have coffee, well He'll find a way! Now, why don't you start preparing breakfast. I think *two* eggs this morning, please."

Oo-lan departed into the kitchen in silence. But before she'd even had time to break the eggs, there was *another* knock at the front door. Ready for anything, Granny Han went to investigate.

There at the door stood a lad from the large boys' school just around the corner. He was holding a big yellow papaya!

"This papaya comes from one of our own trees," he explained. "Mother thought it was

much too nice for us to keep to ourselves, and she wanted you to have it." He thrust the golden fruit into her hands and rode off on his bicycle.

So many answers to prayer in the space of ten minutes ... Granny Han went back inside, rejoicing.

Again Oo-lan was full of questions—how? where? who?

"Mrs. Chang's boy just brought this for me, on his way to school," said Granny Han with a smile. "It comes from their very own tree. Isn't it a beauty?" Now everything was lined up for a real celebration breakfast!

CHAPTER 5

If Anyone is Thirsty

"Thank you, Oo-lan," Granny Han beamed as her house-helper came in with a plate of bread. "What a feast!"

But Oo-lan still looked sullen. "You have no coffee," she complained.

Granny Han looked up at her, her eyes searching the girl's joyless face. Would she never see, never understand the power and love of God?

"Oo-lan," she said, sadly but gently, "if God thinks I should have coffee, He will give me coffee too."

Even as she spoke, there came yet another knock on the front door! This time, Oo-lan decided she would see for herself what was going on, and hurried to the door. Granny Han followed.

The visitor this time turned out to be another

Mrs. Wang from a different part of the city. She had pedalled quite a distance on her bicycle, and Granny Han couldn't understand why she had come so early to see her.

Mrs. Wang smiled at them. "You know, Han Po Po," she began, "my husband is a pilot, and sometimes he flies to Tokyo, Manila, Hong Kong … and often he brings me back a present."

Granny Han waited, not sure what all this had to do with her.

Mrs. Wang triumphantly produced something from her basket. "Just look what he brought me this time!"

Granny Han gasped —in Mrs. Wang's hands was a large jar of instant coffee, an almost unobtainable luxury.

"Do you drink it?" Mrs. Wang inquired politely.

Granny Han was silent. She didn't want to say "yes" and appear greedy, but she certainly didn't want to lie and say "no"!

"No one in our family drinks it," continued Mrs. Wang. "I can't think why my husband brought it. Do *you* like it?"

Granny Han struggled with her conscience. "Mrs. Wang," she said at last, "you should take that coffee down the street to the shop that sells foreign things; they'll give you a good price for it, I'm sure, and then you can use the money to buy other presents for yourself and the children."

"No! No!" insisted Mrs. Wang. "You *do* drink it, don't you?"

Granny Han finally admitted that she did, so Mrs. Wang pressed the jar into her hands, climbed quickly back onto her bicycle and pedalled away.

As they went back into the house, Oo-lan remarked, "Imagine Mrs. Wang liking you so much! That's a really big present. She could have sold it for at least five dollars ..."

Granny Han hardly heard her. She was too

busy marvelling at the loving care of her God, providing for her every need, down to the last detail. With all this wonderful supply, she could have breakfast several times a day for several days!

CHAPTER 6

Loaves and Fishes

Breakfast was one thing—a thousand dollars to pay for the student conference was another! Or was it? God was the same God—faithful, loving and able to meet *every* need.

Granny Han got down on her knees on Wednesday morning. "Lord," she said, "you're the one who can multiply the loaves and the fishes ... all I've got is ten dollars, and I need a thousand by this evening! I ask you to give this ... for your glory."

A few minutes later a telegram arrived from some missionary friends who were on their way home to Hong Kong. Could they all have lunch together? With their four children?

"Oh no!" thought Granny Han. "That's hardly an answer to prayer—whatever can I feed them?" There was hardly any steamed bread left, and no rice at all.

While she was still thinking over this new development, a second telegram arrived.

"I forgot to say," it read, "Go and order the best possible meal from that favorite restaurant of yours—our treat!"

Joyfully Granny Han thanked the Lord—the loaves were beginning to multiply! But the best was yet to come ...

Over lunch, her friend said, "We felt that you had a particular need at the moment, something you're not telling anyone about. Is that true?

Reluctantly, Granny Han told them about the robbery, and how serious the situation now was.

"Well now," said her friend. "Do you know, we'd already decided to give you what's left of our Taiwan money, rather than change it back into Hong Kong money." And he put a fat envelope on the table.

"May I open it?" Slowly, Granny Han counted out—exactly one thousand dollars.

When she arrived at church that evening, the young student leader couldn't hide his anxiety.

"What are we going to do, Han Po Po? We've got to pay the money right after this meeting, and there's no way we can get it."

"Why wait till after the meeting? Give it to them now!" Gleefully, Granny Han pulled the envelope out of her bag and handed it to the astonished young man.

And so the Lord continued to provide for Granny Han. There were gifts of money, jam, a watch, a train ticket, rings—even a box of chocolates!

"What a Father!" thought Granny Han. "Not just my needs supplied, but even extras, like chocolates ..."

But one thing still remained. Oo-lan. Had she been responsible for the robbery, and if so, what did God want Granny Han to do about it?

CHAPTER 7

A Matter of Life and Death

One night Oo-lan didn't come in till two in the morning.

"Where have you been?" asked Granny Han. "I've been worried about you."

Oo-lan was furious. As Granny Han bolted the door, Oo-lan rushed into the house, shut Cinderella the dog into an upstairs room, and grabbed hold of the large meat chopper, raising it ready to strike!

Granny Han tried to play for time, reasoning, preaching, praying ... Just as she felt she couldn't resist another minute, Cinderella finally managed to break free! She dashed down and bit Oo-lan hard in the leg.

The girl screamed with pain and let go of Granny Han, who quickly wrenched the knife from her hands.

Granny Han had to dismiss Oo-lan, and she quickly moved to a new house in case Oo-lan's brother, who was a gangster, tried to get his revenge. How fortunate she did! The following morning the neighbors at the old house reported that a large gang of men had come to the house, and not finding her there, had broken up the house instead ...

Granny Han went on praying for Oo-lan, and asked her friends to pray for her too. But nothing seemed to happen, and eventually she lost all trace of her.

Five years later, at Chinese New Year, a couple rode up to Granny Han's gate on a motorbike. She was amazed to see Oo-lan and her younger brother!

"I've come to confess!" Oo-lan didn't waste time on greetings. "I'm married now, with two little boys—but I can't go on living like this! I've told my husband everything, and now I must tell you. I took your money—I took all sorts of things. If you want to send me to prison, go on, send me! That's where I belong."

Slowly, Granny Han shook her head. "No, your little boys need their mother."

"But I'm not fit to be their mother," sighed Oo-lan.

That day Oo-lan gave her life to God, and her husband wasn't far behind.

"Han Po Po," at last Oo-lan's face was alight with joy. "Truly your God is wonderful!"

Oo-lan and her husband paid back all the money, and today they are still serving God, with their three sons.